THE BEATLES
KEYBOARD BOOK

5 .... ABOUT THIS BOOK

20 .... ALL YOU NEED IS LOVE

6 .... BACK IN THE U.S.S.R.

12 .... BIRTHDAY

16 .... COME TOGETHER

29 .... A DAY IN THE LIFE

36 .... DON'T LET ME DOWN

40 .... GET BACK

52 .... GOOD DAY SUNSHINE

45 .... HELLO, GOODBYE

64 .... HEY JUDE

127 .... I AM THE WALRUS

74 .... LADY MADONNA

68 .... LET IT BE

79 .... THE LONG AND WINDING ROAD

84 .... LUCY IN THE SKY WITH DIAMONDS

86 .... MARTHA MY DEAR

96 .... OB-LA-DI, OB-LA-DA

93 .... OH! DARLING

100 .... PENNY LANE

108 .... REVOLUTION

113 .... WE CAN WORK IT OUT

116 .... WITH A LITTLE HELP FROM MY FRIENDS

138 .... YOU NEVER GIVE ME YOUR MONEY

58 .... YOUR MOTHER SHOULD KNOW

122 .... YOU'RE GOING TO LOSE THAT GIRL

ABOUT THIS BOOK

WHEN PLAYING THROUGH THE TRANSCRIPTIONS IN THIS BOOK, IT IS IMPORTANT TO CONSIDER THE FOLLOWING:

1. THE PRIMARY KEYBOARD PART ALWAYS APPEARS DIRECTLY BELOW THE VOCAL LINE.

2. ANY SECONDARY KEYBOARD PARTS APPEAR BELOW THE PRIMARY KEYBOARD PART. THE INSTRUMENT SOUND IS ALWAYS INDICATED IN THE MEASURE IN WHICH THE PART IS FIRST PLAYED. (SOUND CHANGES ARE ALSO INDICATED WHERE APPROPRIATE.)

3. INSTRUMENTAL PARTS, SUCH AS STRING AND HORN LINES, ARE ALSO INCLUDED THROUGHOUT. IT IS IMPORTANT TO NOTE THAT THESE PARTS ARE *ARRANGED* SO THAT THEY MAY BE PLAYED AS SECONDARY KEYBOARD PARTS. THE PITCHES ARE ACCURATE, HOWEVER, THE VOICINGS OF THE CHORDS MAY BE MODIFIED SO THAT THEY ARE MORE INDICATIVE OF A KEYBOARD APPROACH.

4. IF THERE IS NO KEYBOARD PART ON THE RECORDING (FOR AN EXTENDED TIME), OTHER INSTRUMENTAL PARTS ARE OFTEN ARRANGED TO BE PLAYED BY THE PRIMARY KEYBOARD, AND ARE INDICATED AS CUE NOTES. THESE ARE OPTIONAL AND ARE INTENDED TO BE PLAYED ONLY IF THE ACTUAL INSTRUMENTS (SUCH AS GUITAR) ARE NOT AVAILABLE.

5. "FILL" BOXES ARE SOMETIMES INCLUDED WHEN A PARTICULAR FILL, OR FIGURE, IS PLAYED ON THE REPEAT OR D.S. ONLY. A TYPICAL INDICATION WOULD BE "2ND TIME-PLAY FILL 2".

THE TRANSCRIPTIONS IN THIS BOOK ARE USABLE IN A VARIETY OF SITUATIONS: WITH A BAND; WITH A SEQUENCER; WITH A TAPE RECORDER; OR SOLO PLAYING. WHATEVER YOUR PURPOSE IS, YOU CAN NOW PLAY YOUR FAVORITE SONGS JUST AS THE ARTISTS RECORDED THEM.

Back In The U.S.S.R.

Words and Music by John Lennon and Paul McCartney

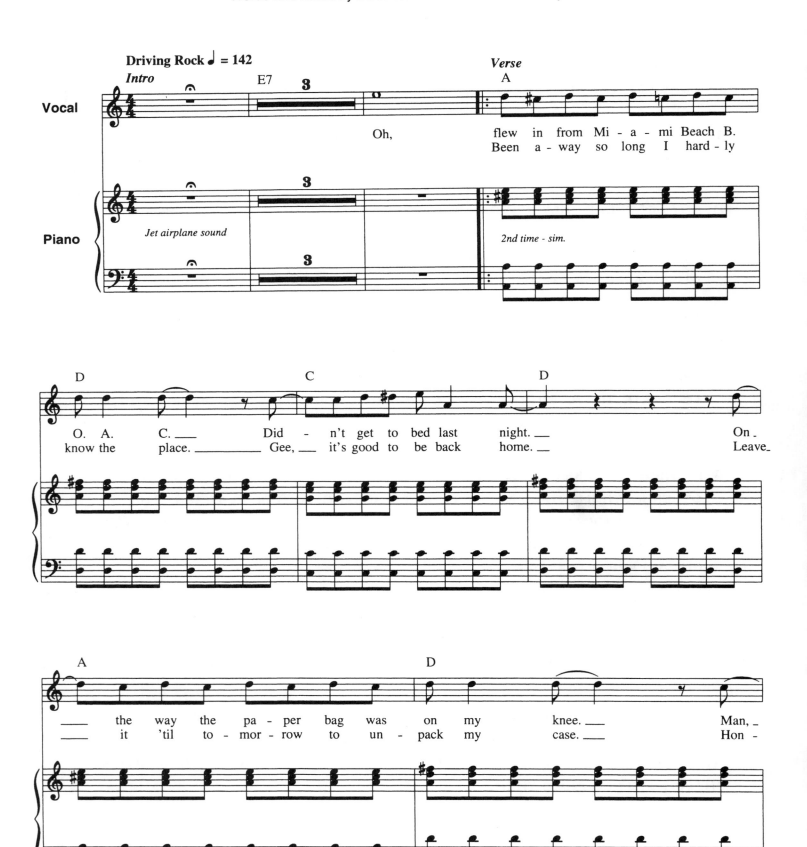

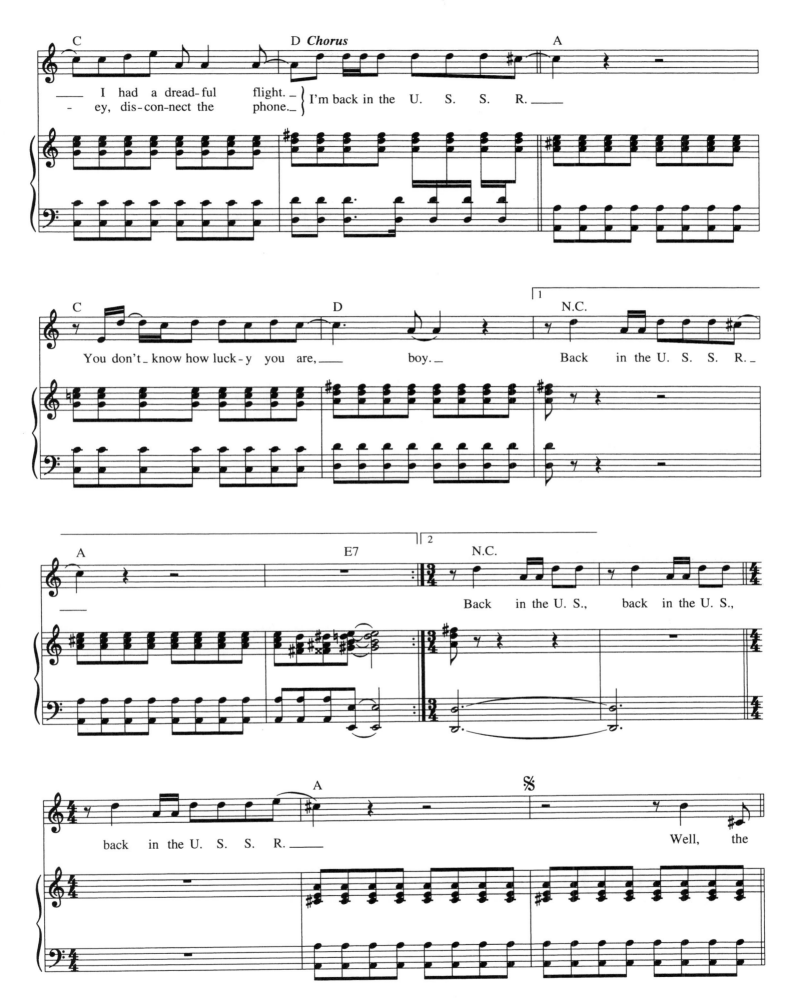

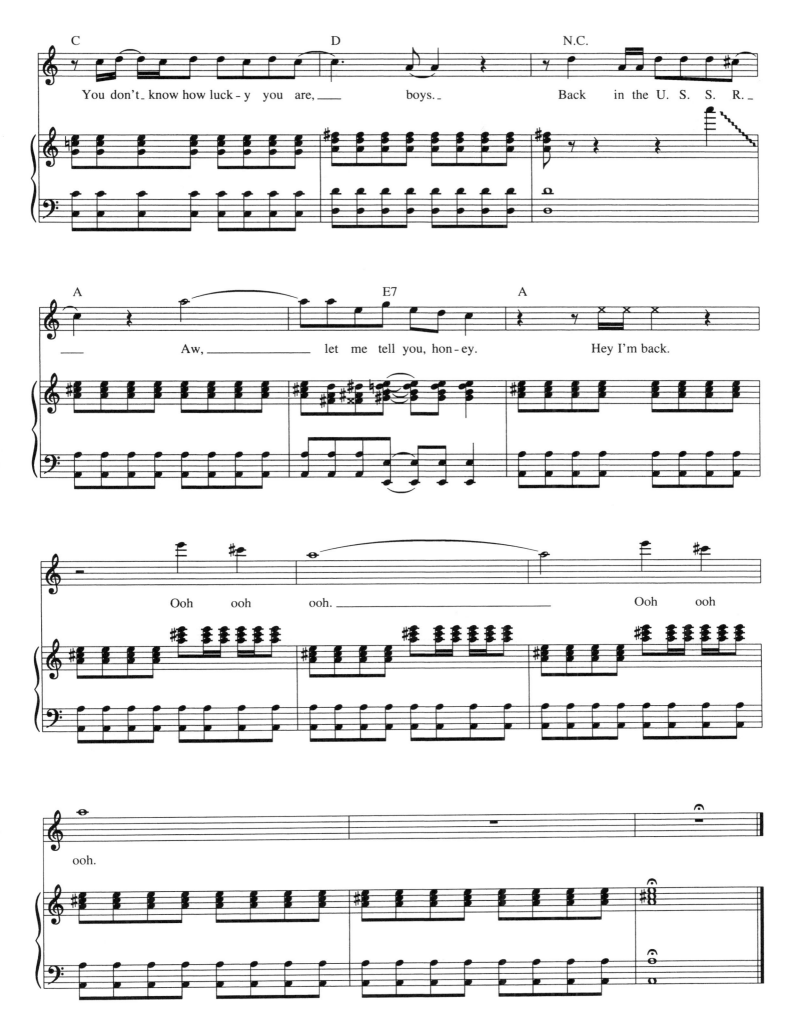

Birthday

Words and Music by John Lennon and Paul McCartney

*Guitar and Bass play same figure as in Intro

Come Together

Words and Music by John Lennon and Paul McCartney

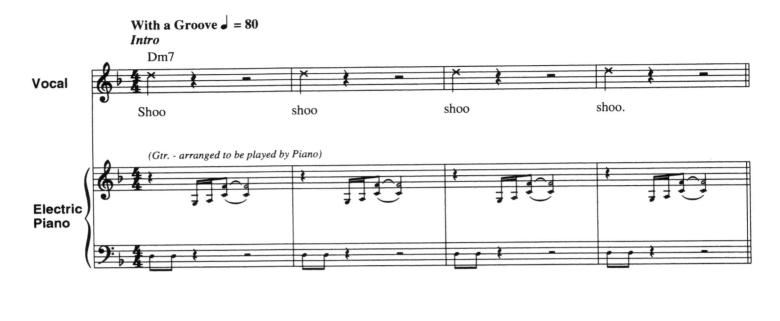

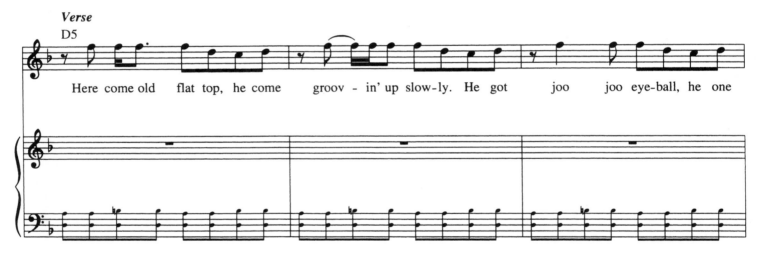

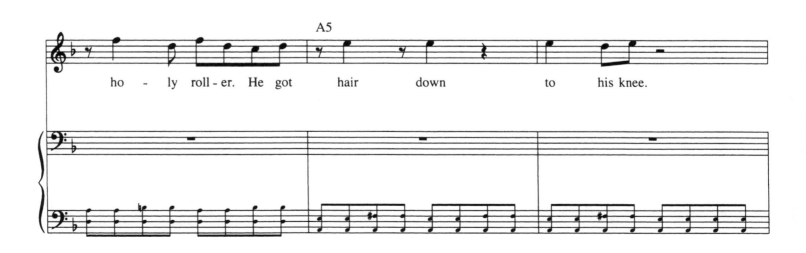

19

All You Need Is Love

Words and Music by John Lennon and Paul McCartney

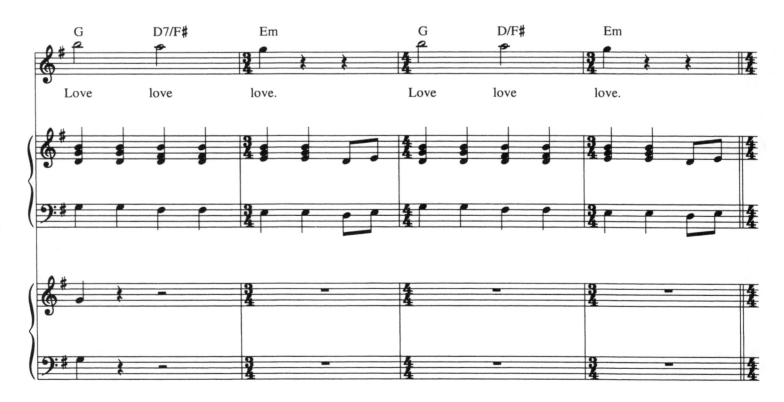

Love   love   love.

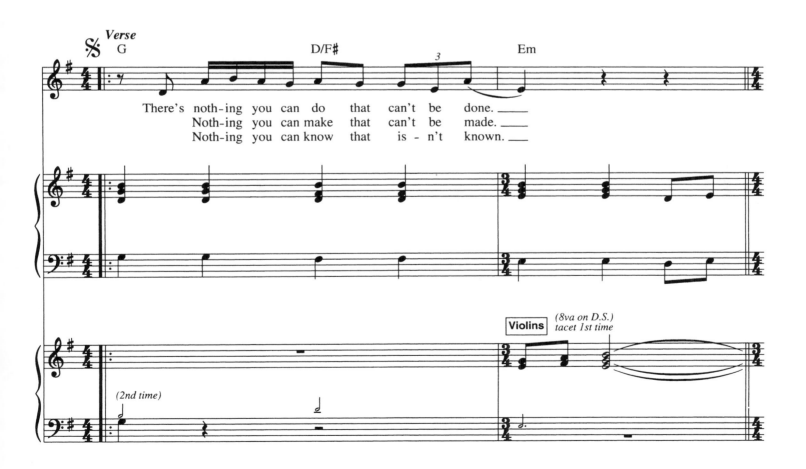

Verse

There's noth-ing you can do   that   can't   be   done. ___
Noth-ing you can make   that   can't   be   made. ___
Noth-ing you can know   that   is - n't   known. ___

Violins *(8va on D.S.)* *tacet 1st time*

(2nd time)

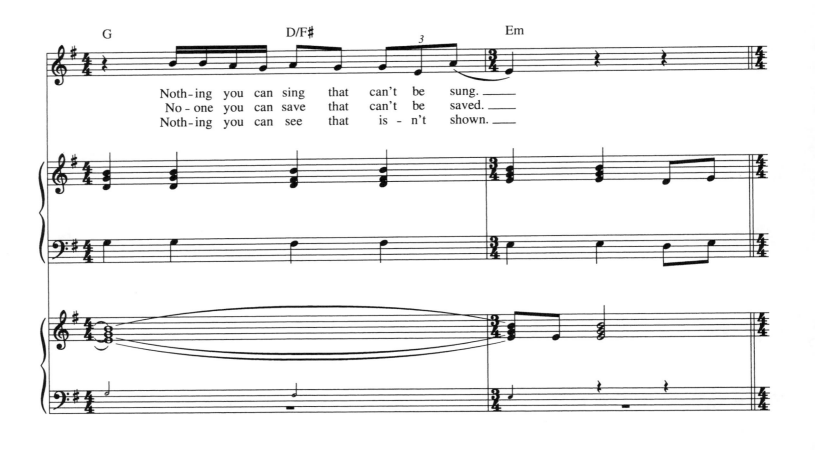

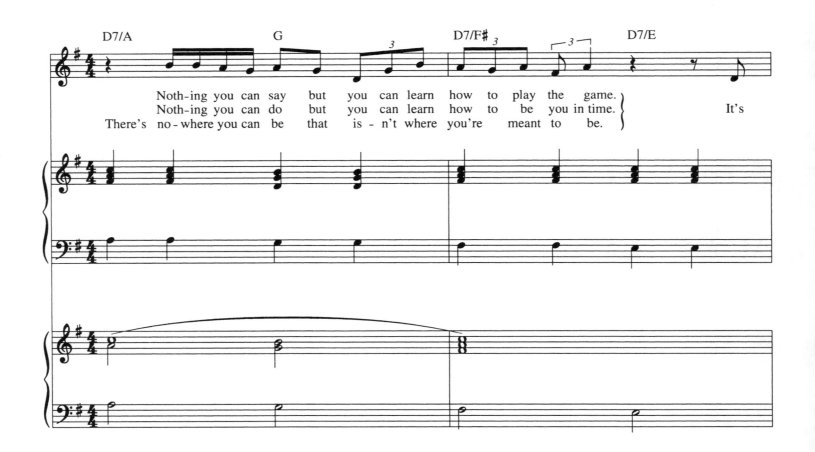

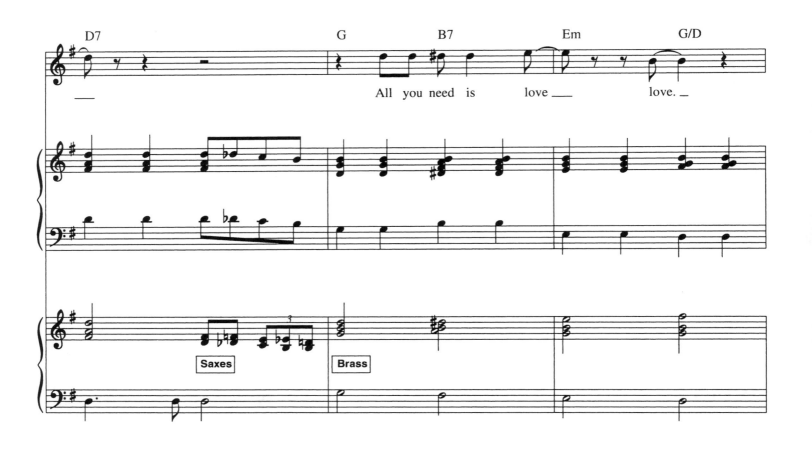

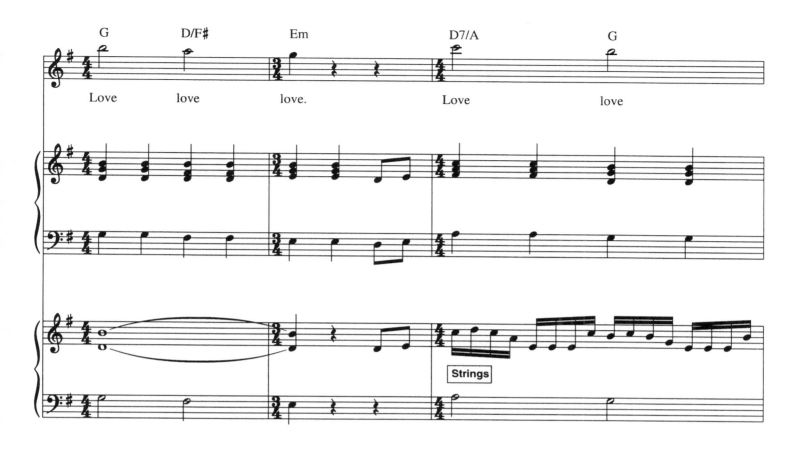

Love   love   love.   Love   love

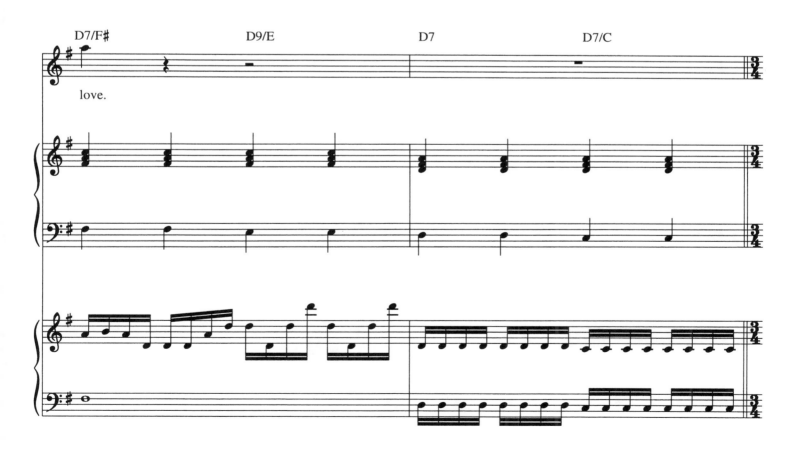

love.

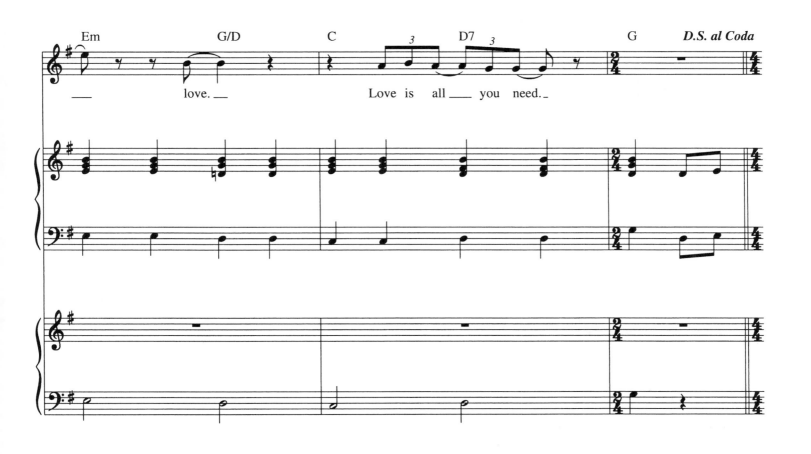

love. ___

Love is all ___ you need. _

All you need is love. ___ *(Spoken:) All together now.*

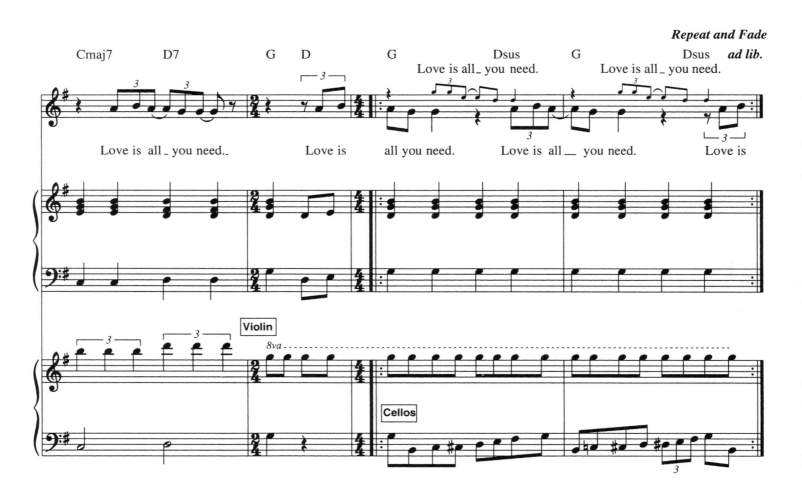

A Day In The Life

Words and Music by John Lennon and Paul McCartney

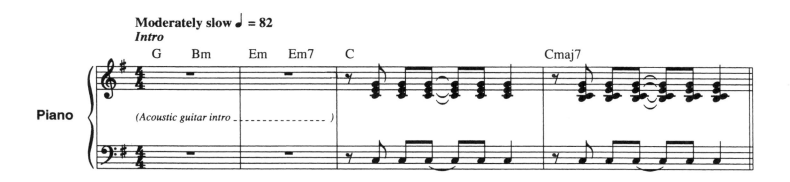

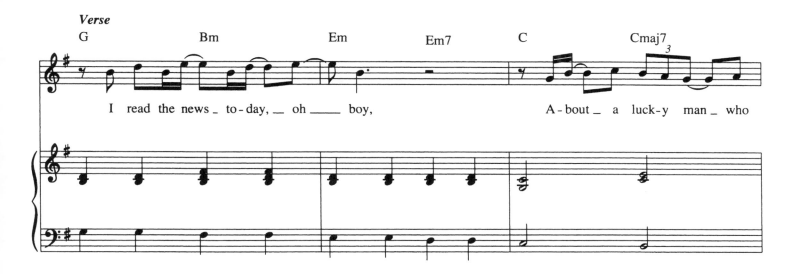

E

up and cresc.

Bridge

Woke up,   fell out of bed,   dragged a   comb a-cross my head.

D   E   B9   E   B9

Found my way down-stairs and drank a cup.   And look-ing up_   I no-ticed I was late.

35

Don't Let Me Down

Words and Music by John Lennon and Paul McCartney

Don't let me down. _____

Don't let me

down. _____

To Coda ⊕ *Bridge*

I'm in love for the first _ time.

Don't you know_ it's gon-na last.

It's a love_ that lasts_ for-ev-

er.

It's a love_ that has _ no_____ past.

D.S. al Coda
Chorus

Don't let me

Get Back

Words and Music by John Lennon and Paul McCartney

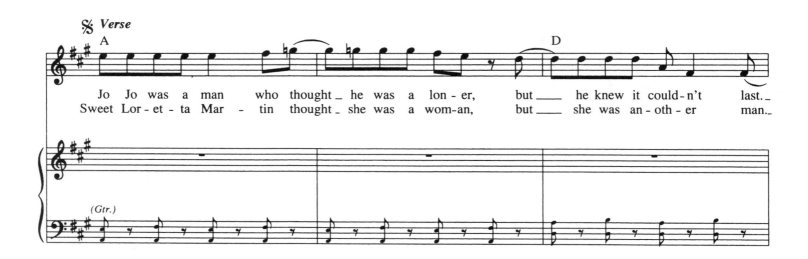

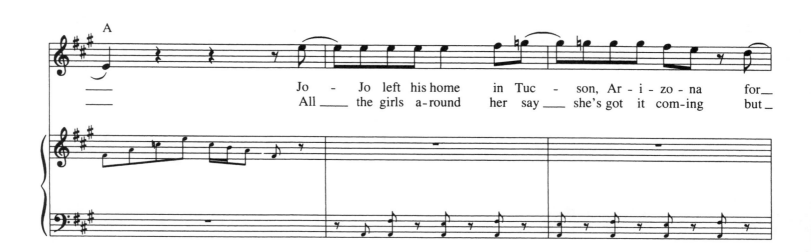

(Spoken:) Go Home

Get back,_

Chorus

Get back, ___ back ___ to where you once be - longed. ___

Get back, ___ Get back, ___ back._

___ to where you once be - longed. ___ Get back Jo.

R.H.

Hello, Goodbye

Words and Music by John Lennon and Paul McCartney

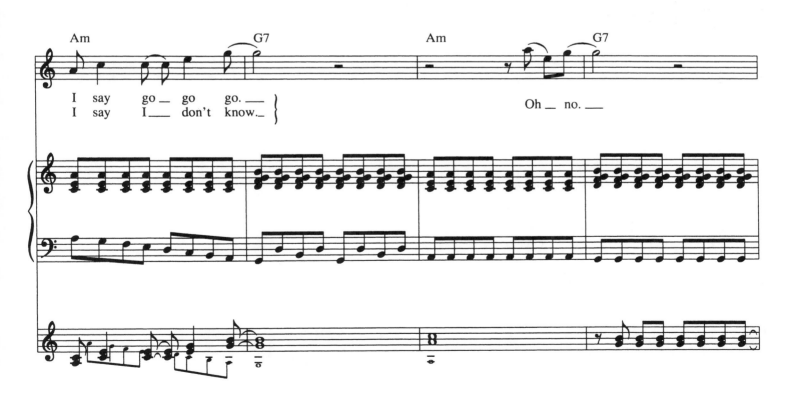

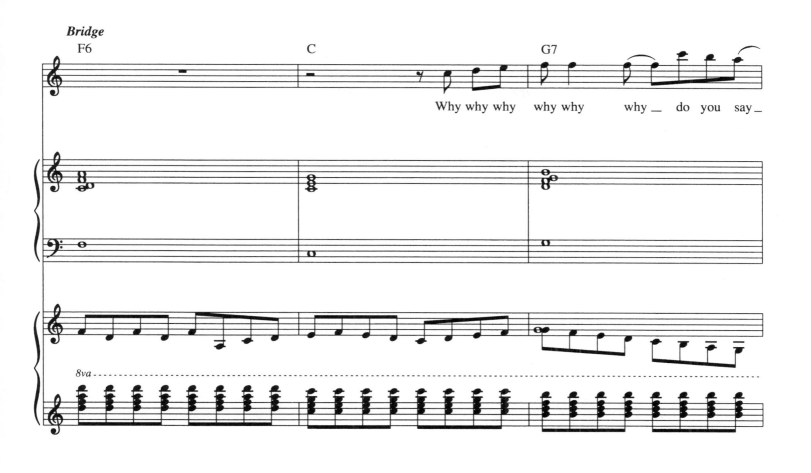

Bridge

Why why why why why why __ do you say __

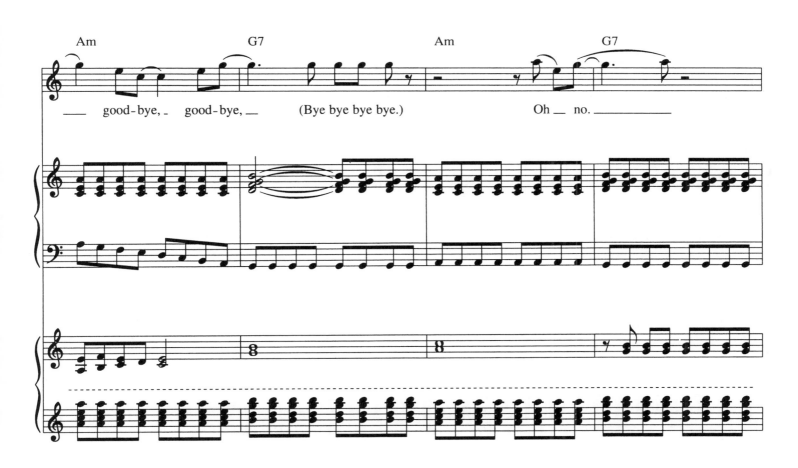

__ good-bye, __ good-bye, __ (Bye bye bye bye.) Oh __ no. _____

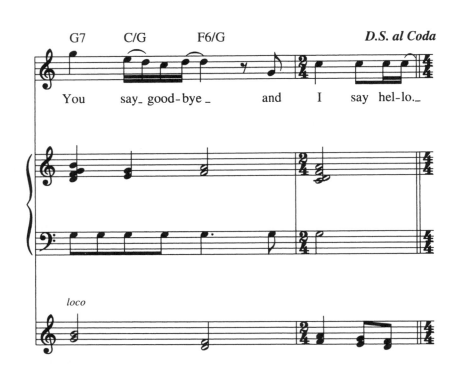

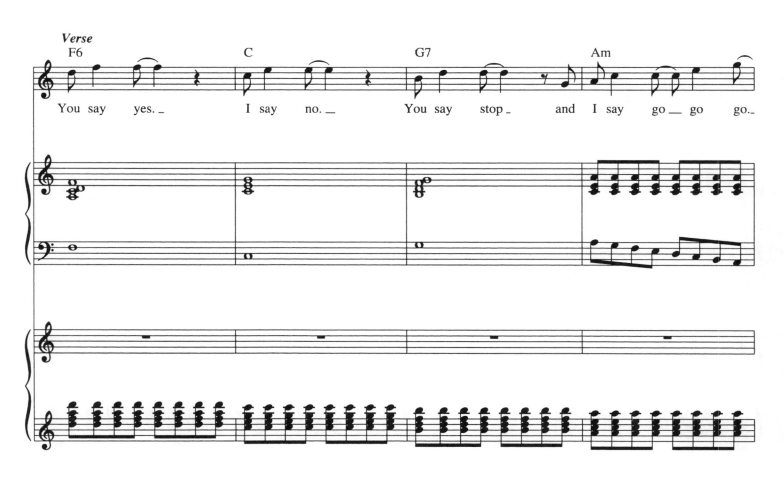

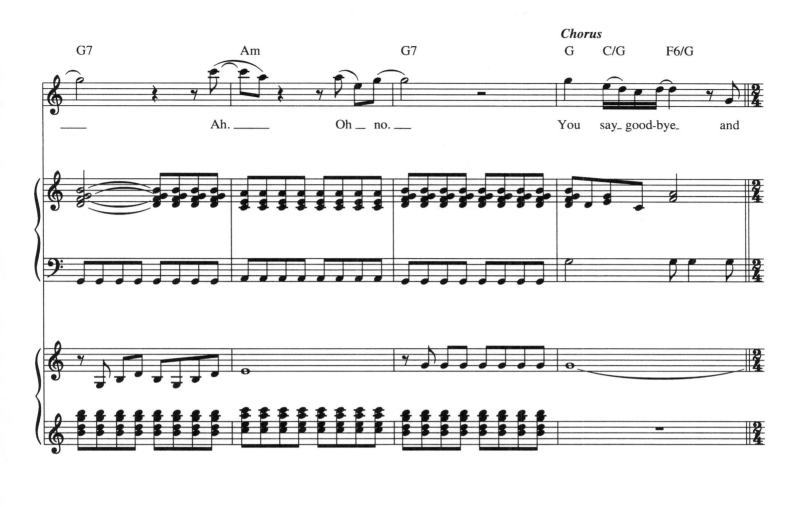

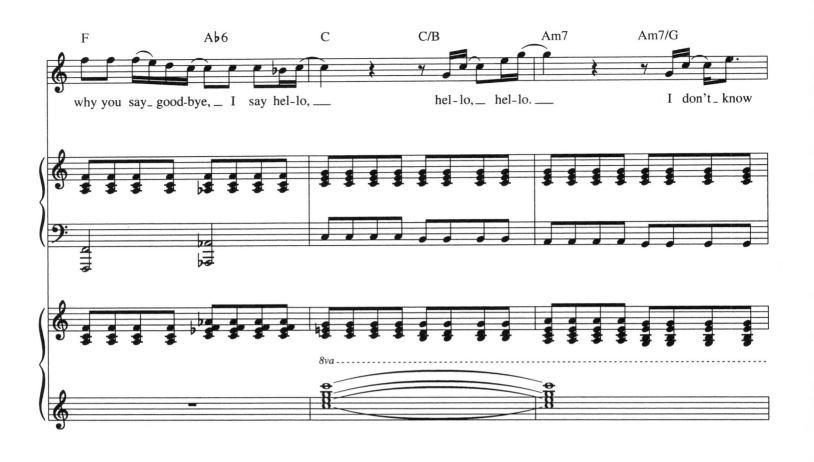

why you say_ good-bye, _ I say hel-lo, _____ hel-lo, _ hel-lo. _____ I don't_ know

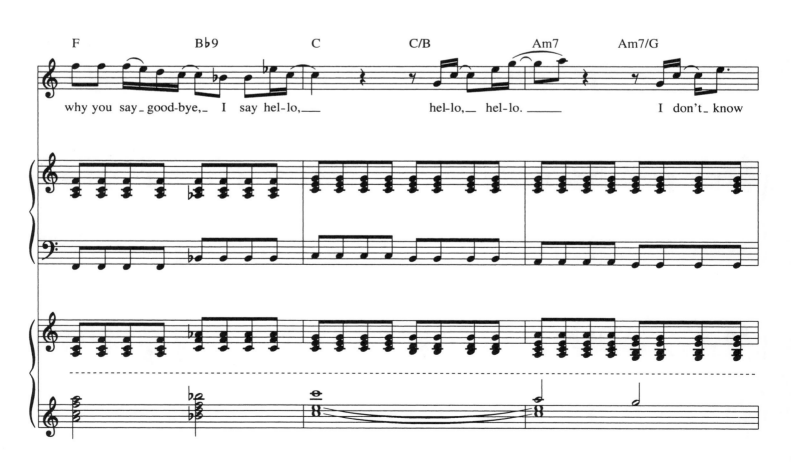

why you say_ good-bye, _ I say hel-lo, _____ hel-lo, _ hel-lo. _____ I don't_ know

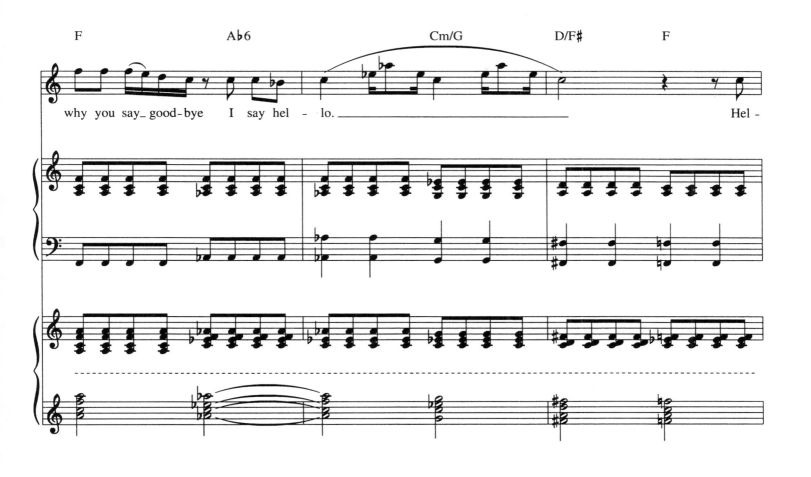

why you say_ good-bye I say hel - lo. _____ Hel -

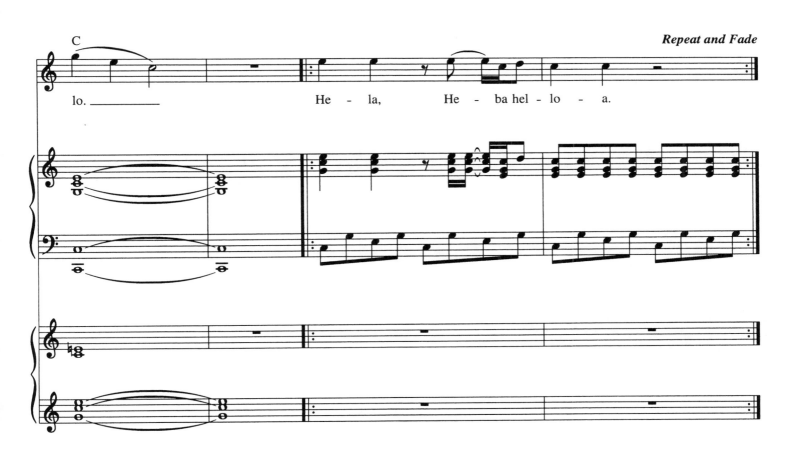

lo. _____ He - la, He - ba hel - lo - a.

Repeat and Fade

Good Day Sunshine

Words and Music by John Lennon and Paul McCartney

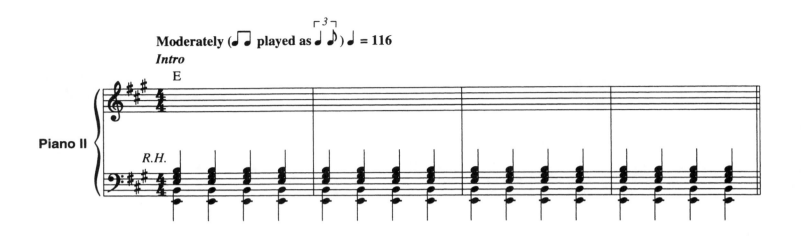

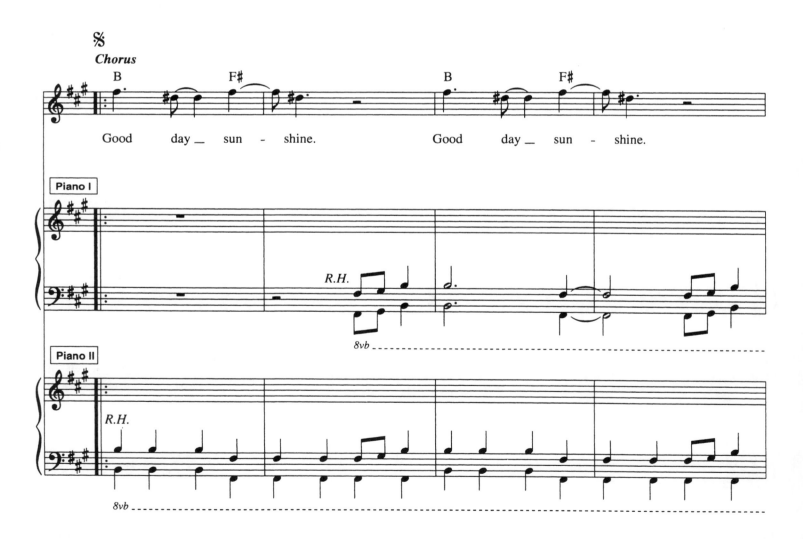

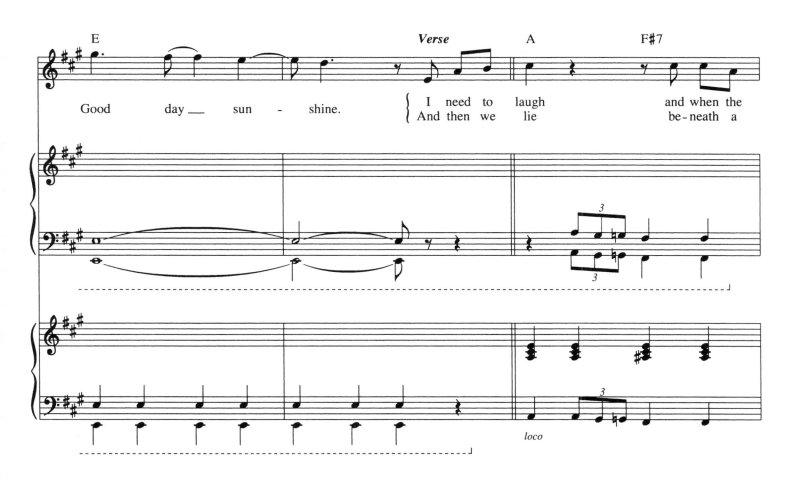

Good day ___ sun - shine.

I need to laugh
And then we lie

and when the
be - neath a

sun is out ___
shad - y tree. ___

I've got some-thing I can laugh a - bout. I feel good ___
I love her and she's lov-ing me. She feels good, ___

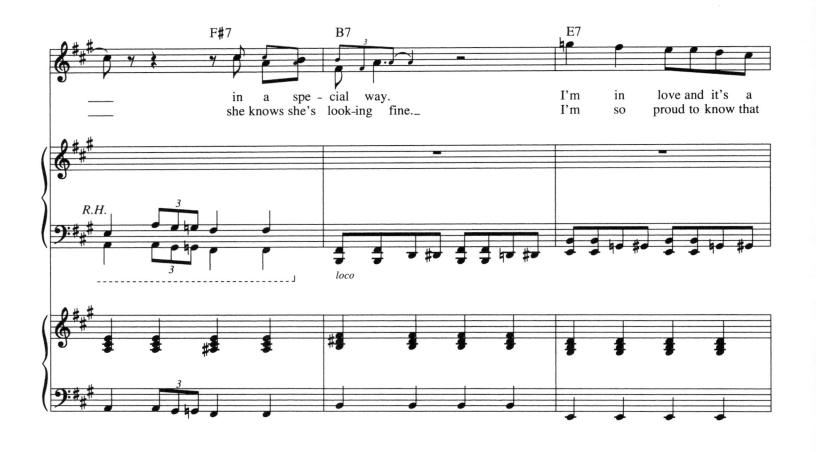

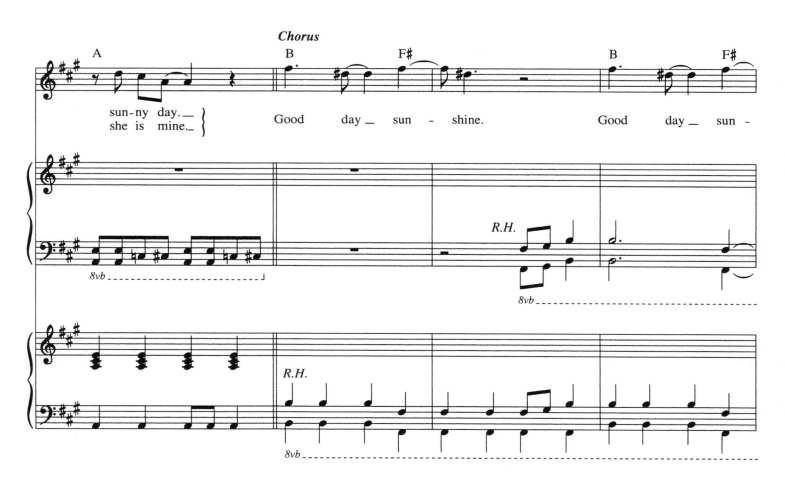

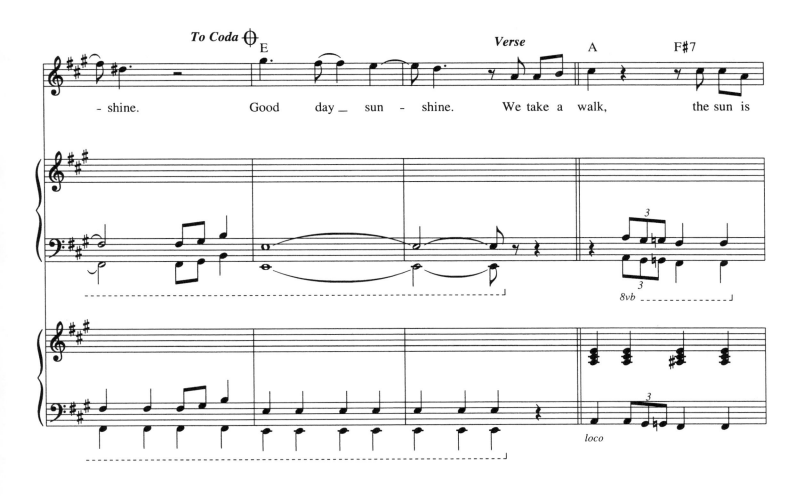

shine. Good day sunshine. We take a walk, the sun is

shin-ing down. Burns my feet as they touch the ground.

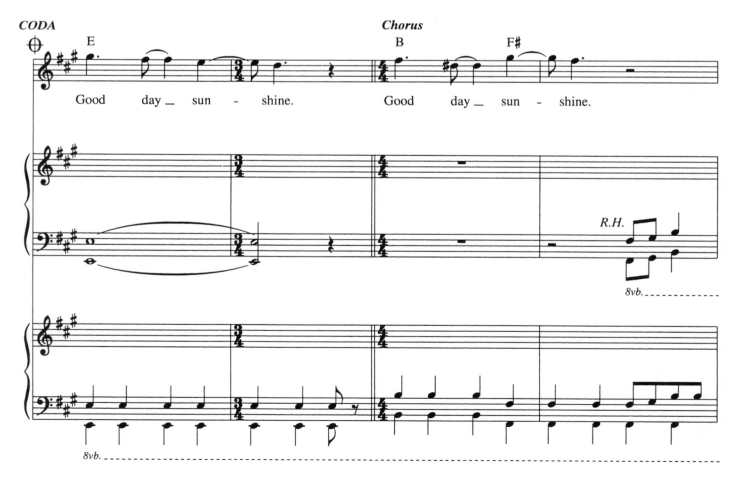

Good day __ sun - shine. Good day __ sun - shine.

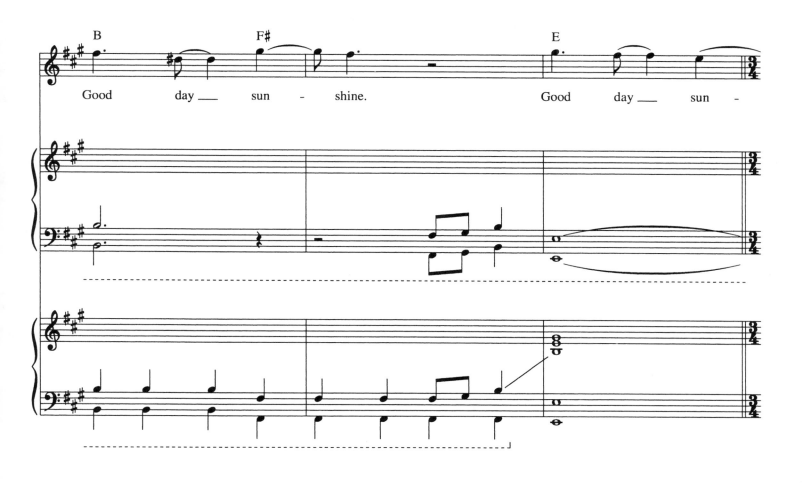

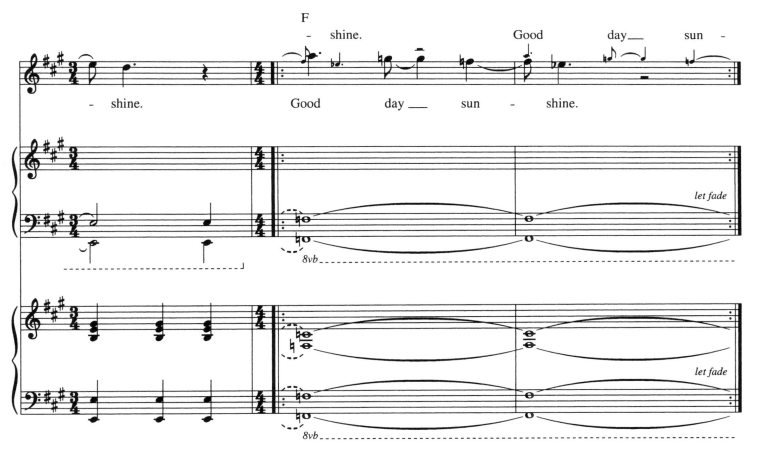

Your Mother Should Know

Words and Music by John Lennon and Paul McCartney

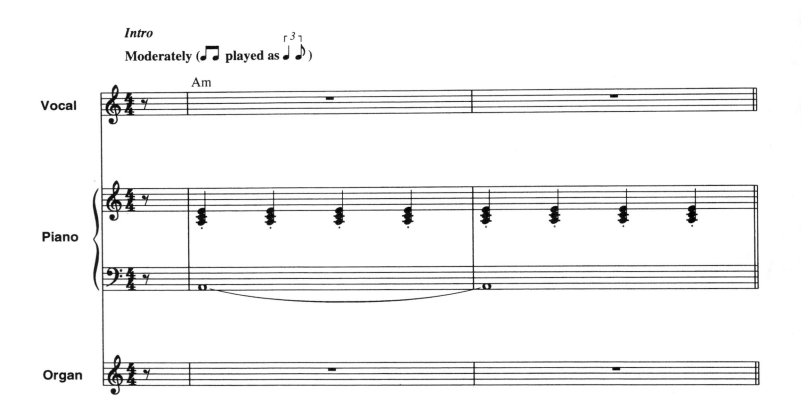

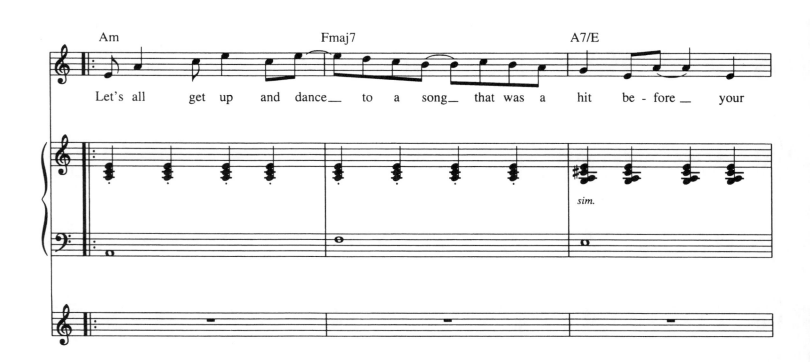

Lift up your hearts and sing ___ me a song ___ that was a
Da da da da da da ___ da da da da da da

Play on D.S. only

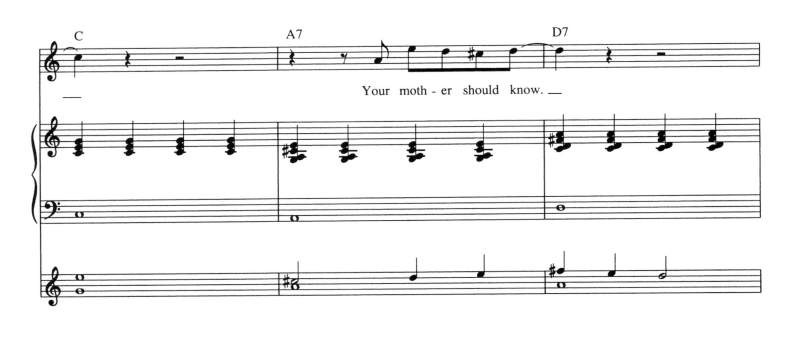

Your moth- er should know. —

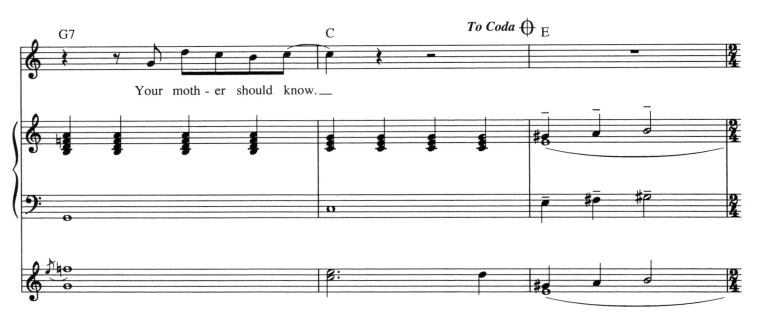

Your moth- er should know. —

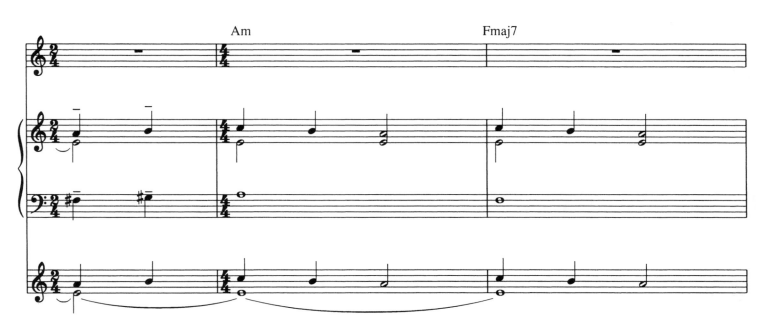

Hey Jude

Words and Music by John Lennon and Paul McCartney

Let It Be

Words and Music by John Lennon and Paul McCartney

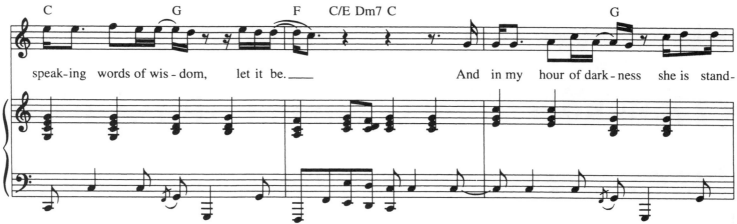

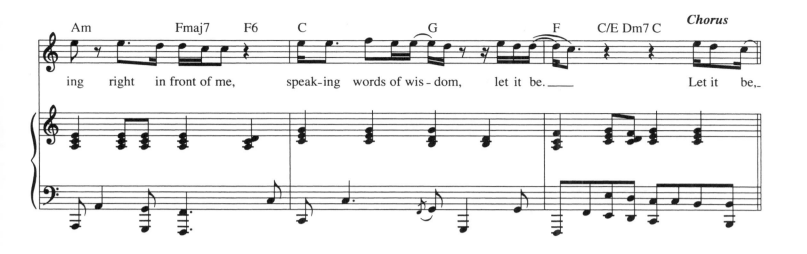

ing right in front of me, speak-ing words of wis - dom, let it be.____ Let it be,_

____ let it be, let it be,____ let it be._ Whis-per words_of wis-dom, let it be._

Organ

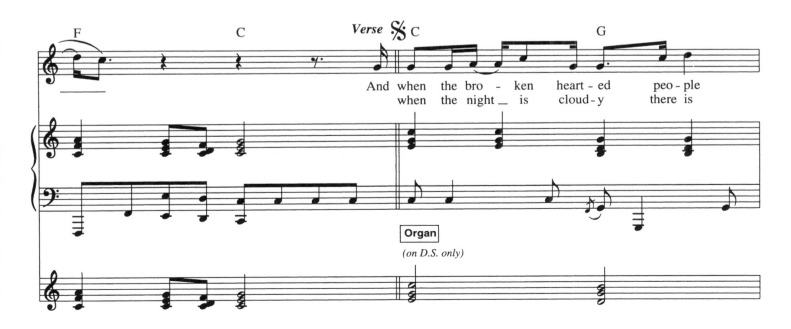

And when the bro - ken heart - ed peo - ple
when the night__ is cloud-y there is

Organ
(on D.S. only)

Lady Madonna

Words and Music by John Lennon and Paul McCartney

Tues - day af - ter - noon __ is nev - er end -

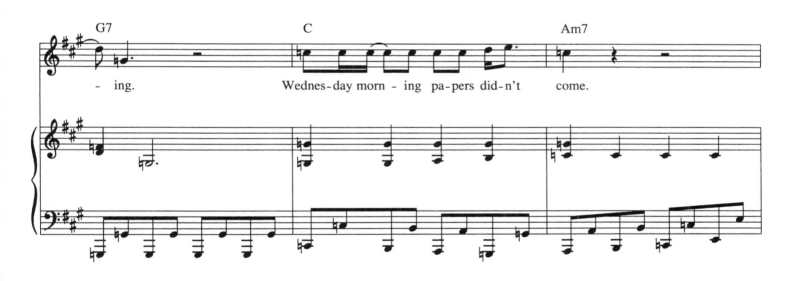

- ing. Wednes - day morn - ing pa - pers did - n't come.

Thurs - day night _ your stock - ings need - ed mend - ing. __ See how they

The Long And Winding Road

Words and Music by John Lennon and Paul McCartney

79

It al-ways leads _ me here, leads me to your door.

Verse
(1.) The wild and wind-y night _ that the rain _ washed a-way _
(2., D.S.) still they lead me back _ to the long _ wind-ing road. _

has left a   pool of   tears ___   cry - ing for   the   day.__

You left me   stand-ing here ___   a   long   long   time   a - go.

Why   leave   me   stand - ing here?

Don't   {leave} me   wait - ing here.

        {keep}

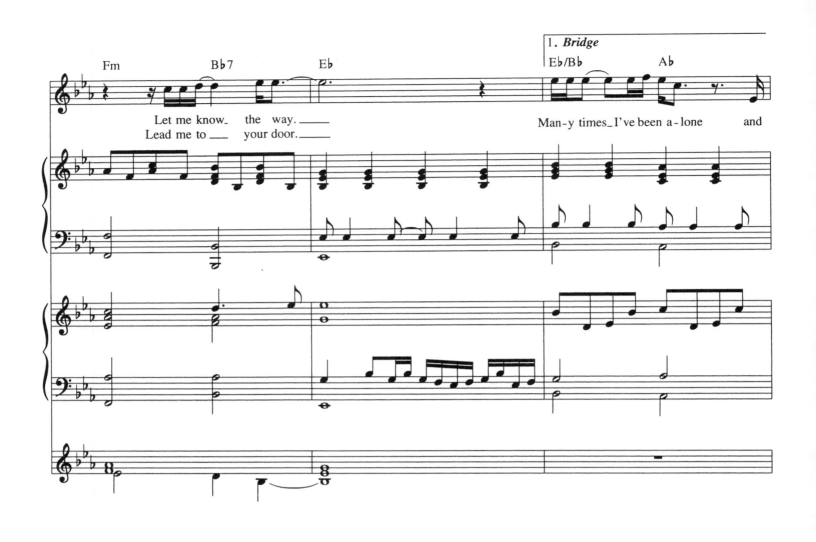

Let me know_ the way._____
Lead me to ___ your door._____

Man-y times_ I've been a-lone   and

man-y times_ I've cried._   An-y-way   you'll nev-er know   the   man-y times_ I've tried._   And

But

Lead me to your _____ door. _____ Yeah yeah yeah   yeah. _

Lucy In The Sky With Diamonds

Words and Music by John Lennon and Paul McCartney

Martha My Dear

Words and Music by John Lennon and Paul McCartney

Mar - tha,_ my dear, though I spend _ my days in con-ver-sa - tion please re-mem-ber

me. Mar-tha, my love, don't for-get me. Mar-tha, my dear.

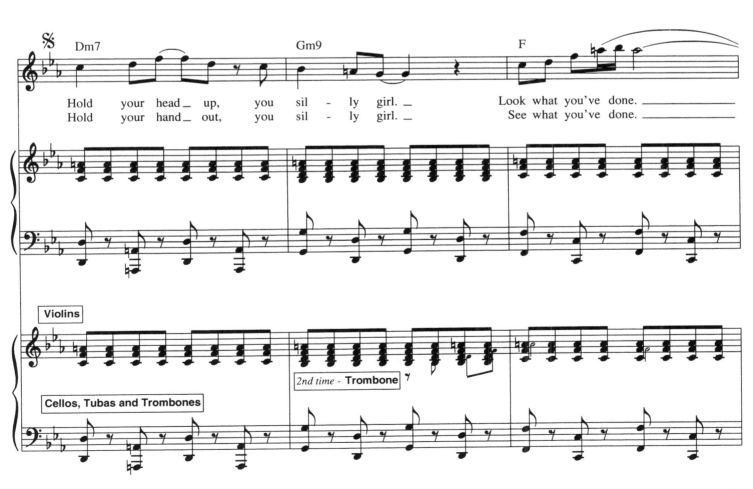

Hold your head up, you sil - ly girl. Look what you've done.
Hold your hand out, you sil - ly girl. See what you've done.

Violins

Cellos, Tubas and Trombones

2nd time - **Trombone**

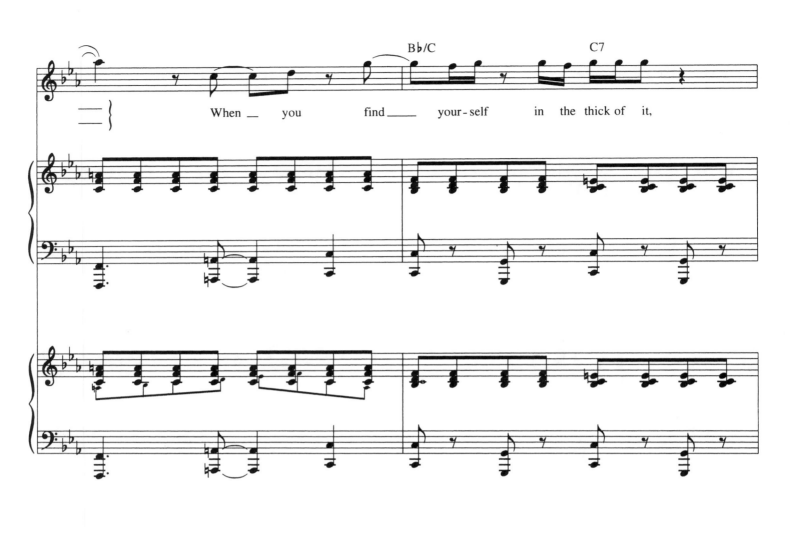

When __ you find ____ your-self in the thick of it,

Help your-self to a bit of what is all a-round _ you, Sil-ly girl. _ Take a

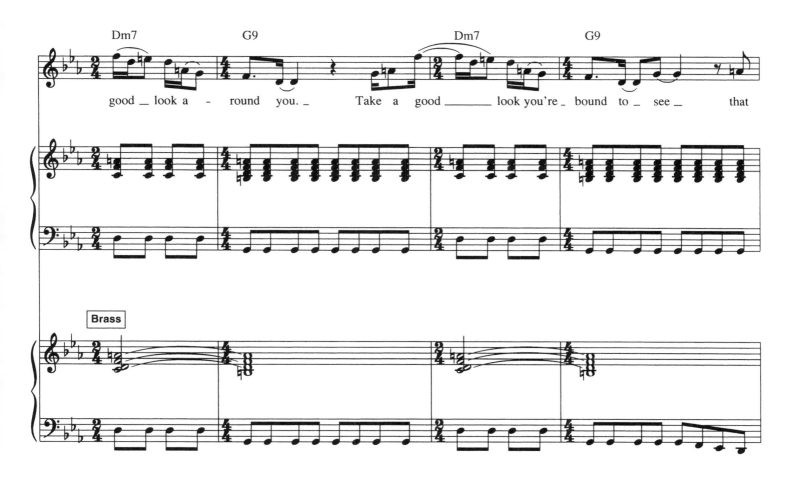

good _ look a - round you. _ Take a good _____ look you're _ bound to _ see _ that

you and me _ _____ were meant to _ be _ for each oth - er, _____ sil - ly girl. _

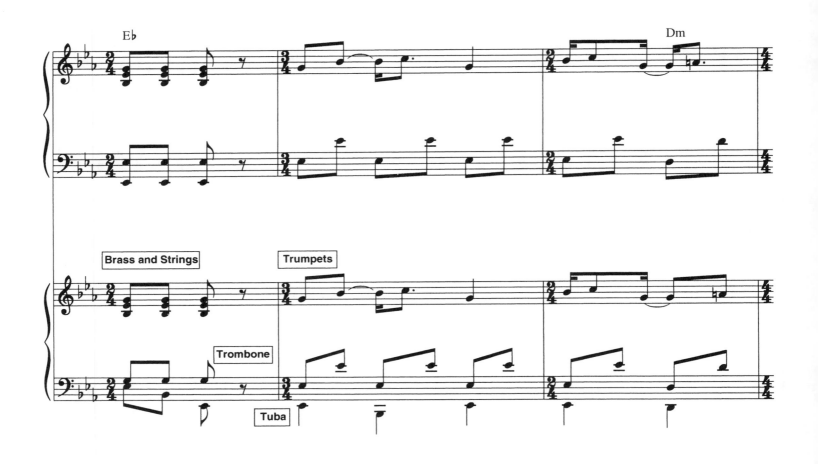

been my in-spi-ra - tion.   Please   be good to me.   Mar-tha, my_ love._   Don't for-get_ me,_

_   Mar - tha, my_ dear. ___

Oh! Darling

Words and Music by John Lennon and Paul McCartney

need me an-y-more, oh well you know I near - ly broke_down and

cried._____ When you told me you did-n't need me an-y-more, Well, you

know I near - ly broke_down and died._____ Oh __ died._____ Oh __

harm._____

Ob-La-Di, Ob-La-Da

Words and Music by John Lennon and Paul McCartney

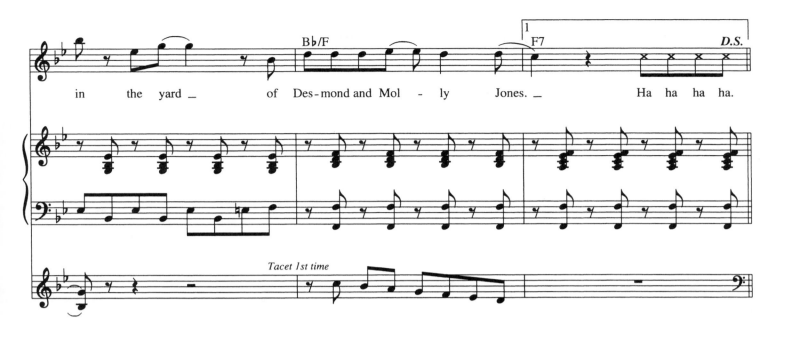

in the yard __ of Des-mond and Mol - ly Jones. __ Ha ha ha ha.

Tacet 1st time

__ Hey, __ hap -

CODA

__ And if you

want some fun __ take ob - la - di - bla - da. Thank you.

Penny Lane

Words and Music by John Lennon and Paul McCartney

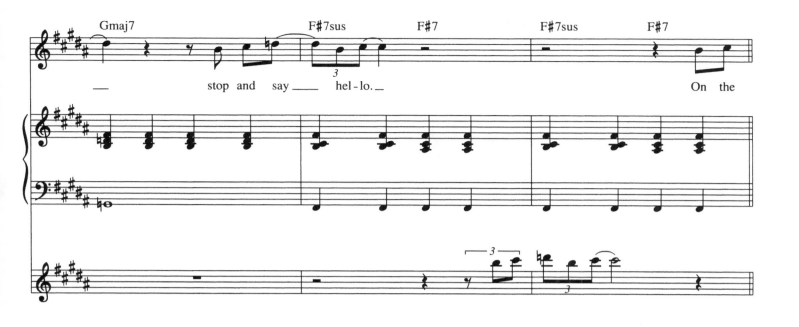

stop and say _____ hel - lo. _

On the

Verse

cor - ner is a bank - er with a mo - tor car.
The bar - ber shaves an - oth - er cus - tom - er.

The lit - tle chil - dren laugh at him _ be - hind his
We see the bank - er sit - ting wait - ing for a

(2nd time - 8va)

Brass

on D.S.S. only

Strings

on D.S.S. only

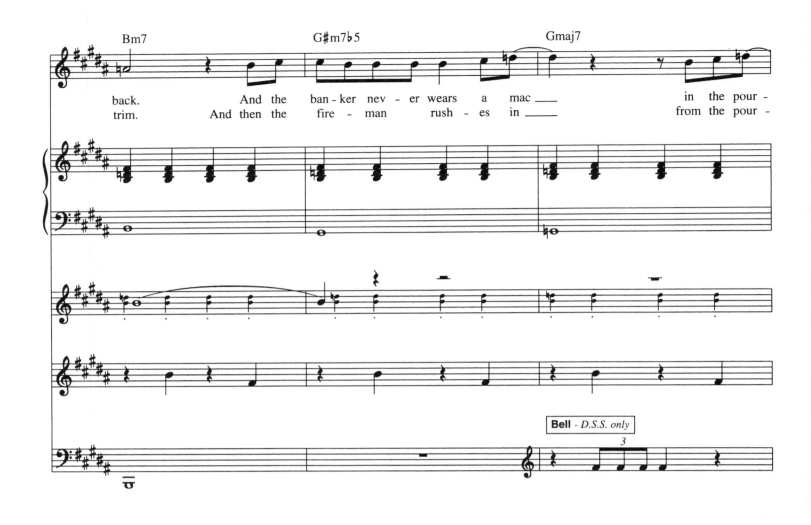

back.　　　　　And the ban - ker nev - er wears a mac ___　　　　in the pour -
trim.　　　　And then the fire - man rush - es in ___　　　　from the pour -

Bell - *D.S.S. only*

- ing rain.　　　　Ver - y strange. _　　Pen - ny Lane ___　　is in my ears _
- ing rain.　　　　Ver - y strange. _　　Pen - ny Lane ___　　is in my ears _

Chorus

(Cues on D.S.S. only)

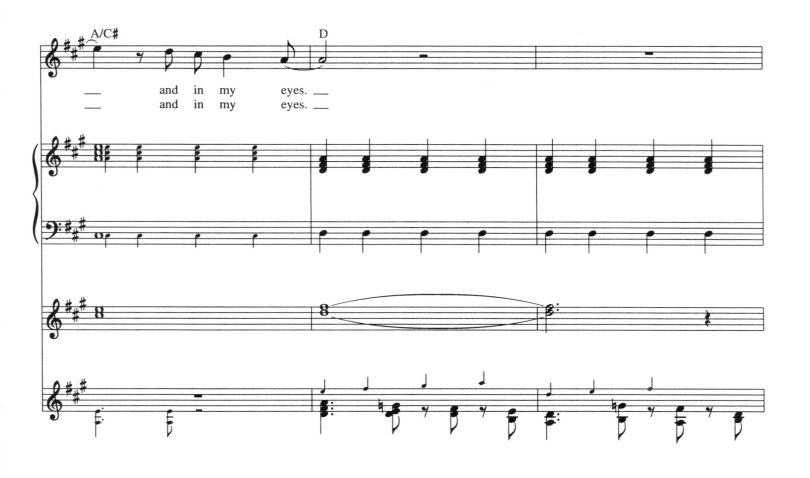

and in my eyes.
and in my eyes.

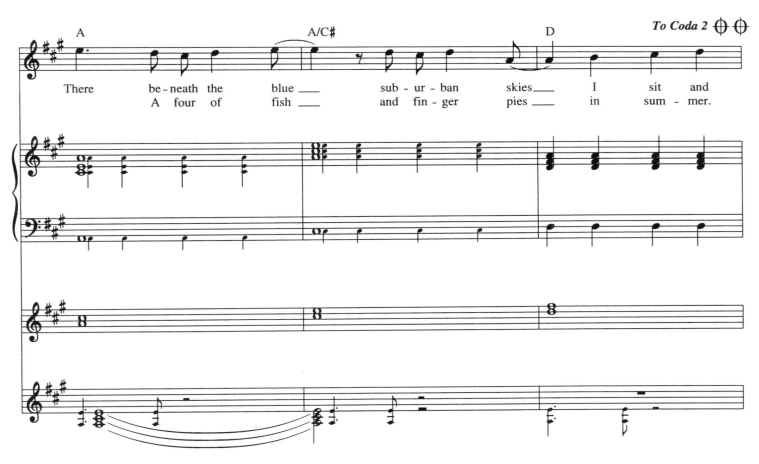

There be-neath the blue ___ sub - ur - ban skies ___ I sit and
A four of fish ___ and fin - ger pies ___ in sum - mer.

To Coda 2

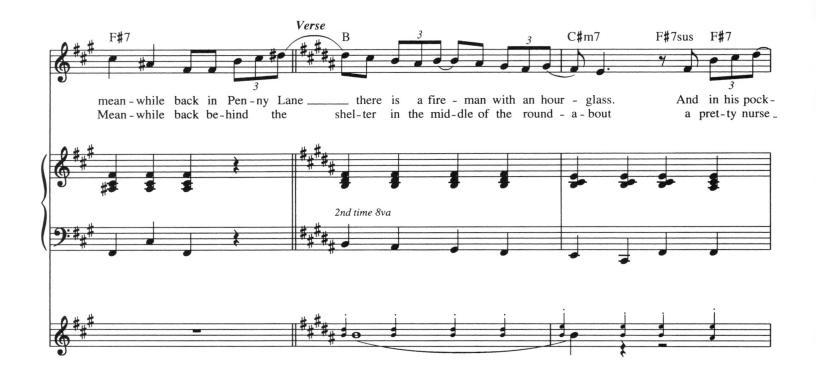

mean-while back in Pen-ny Lane _____ there is a fire-man with an hour-glass.
Mean-while back be-hind the shel-ter in the mid-dle of the round-a-bout

And in his pock-
a pret-ty nurse _

- et is a por-trait of the Queen. _
- is sell-ing pup-pies from a tray. _

He likes to keep his fi-re en-gine clean. _
And though she feels as if she's in a play, _

Tacet 1st time

It's a clean _ ma-chine. _
she is an - y-way. _

Ah. _____

Bell

1st time only

1st time

Bridge

Ah. _____

Piccolo Tpt.

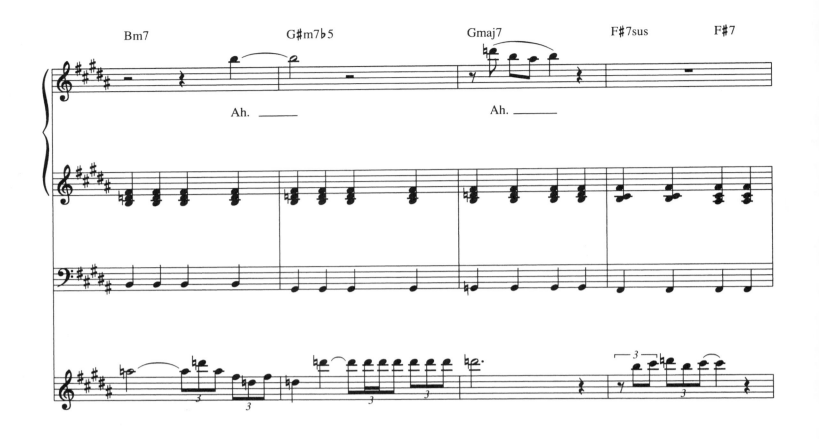

Revolution

Words and Music by John Lennon and Paul McCartney

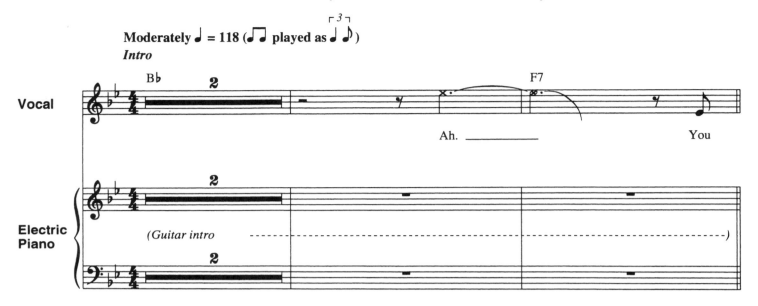

112

We Can Work It Out

Words and Music by John Lennon and Paul McCartney

I have al - ways thought __ that it's a crime. __

So I will ask you once a -

gain. gain.

D.S. al Coda

CODA

We can work it out. __

We can work it out. ____

With A Little Help From My Friends

Words and Music by John Lennon and Paul McCartney

at first sight?___ Yes, I'm cer - tain that it hap-pens all the time.___

What do you see ____ when you turn ____ out the light?___ I can't tell ___

___ you but I know___ it's mine. ___ Oh, ___ I get by ___

Oh, ___ I get by ____ with a lit - tle help ___ from my friends. ___

120

You're Going To Lose That Girl

Words and Music by John Lennon and Paul McCartney

Watch what you do. ____

tak-ing her a-way from you. ____ *Yeah.* ____

To Coda ⊕

The way you treat her, *what else can I do?* ____

(Guitar Solo)

You're gon - na

lose that girl. ____

I Am The Walrus

Words and Music by John Lennon and Paul McCartney

you are me and we are all to-geth-er._____
don't you think the jok-er laughs at you?_____

See how they run like pigs from a gun, see how __ they fly. ____
See how they smile like pigs in a sty, see how __ they snied. __

I'm
I'm

Fr. Horns
(1st time only)

cry - ing. __
cry - ing. __

Sit - ting on a corn - flake,
Sem - o - li - na pil - chard

Strings
(2nd time only)

(1st time only)

waiting for the van to come.
climbing up the Eiffel Tower.

Corporation tee-shirt, stupid bloody Tuesday, man, ___ you been a naughty boy; ___ you let your face grow
Elementary penguin singing Hare Krishna. Man, ___ you should have seen them kicking Edgar Allan

long.
Poe.

I am the eggman, they are the

drip-ping from a dead dog's eye. ____

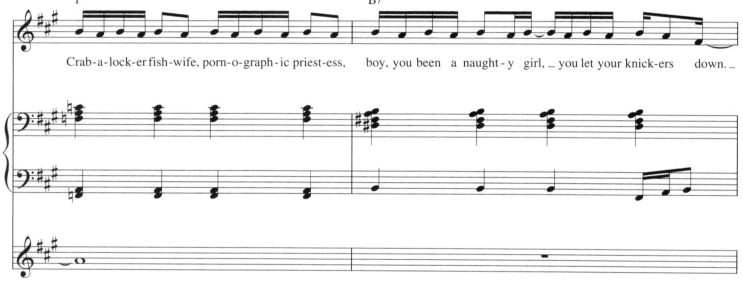

Crab-a-lock-er fish-wife, porn-o-graph-ic priest-ess, boy, you been a naught-y girl, _ you let your knick-ers down. _

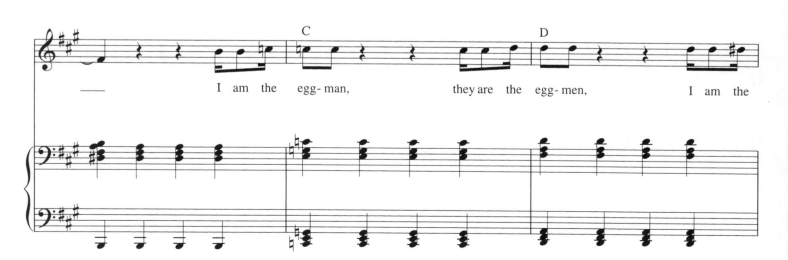

____ I am the egg-man, they are the egg-men, I am the

wal - rus, Goo goo g' - joob.

(alarm clock)

Strings

Sit - ting in an Eng - lish gar -

- den, wait - ing for the sun. _____ If the sun don't

come, you get a tan from stand-ing in the Eng-lish rain. __ I am the

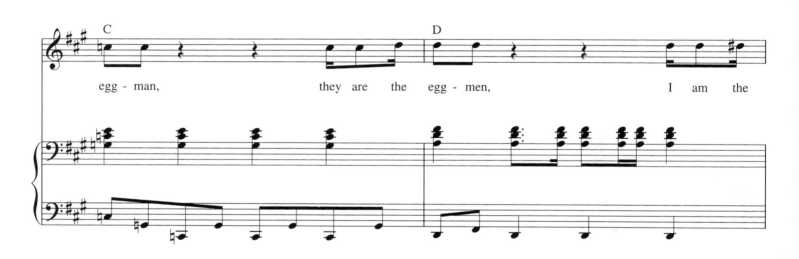

egg - man, they are the egg - men, I am the

D.S. al Coda

wal - rus. Goo goo g' - joob, goo goo __ goo g' - joob.

CODA

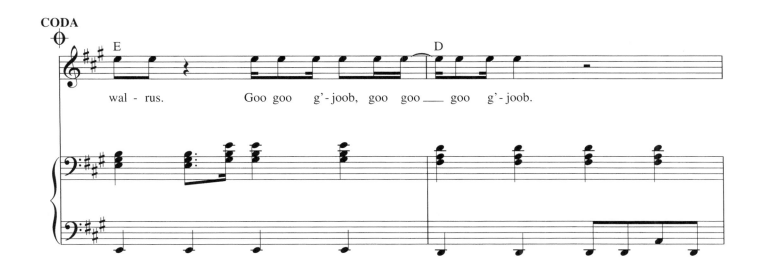

wal - rus.   Goo goo g' - joob, goo goo ___ goo g' - joob.

Goo goo g' - joob goo goo ___ goo g' - joob   goo. ___   Choo-ga choo-ga choo-ga   choo-ga choo-ga choo-ga

Gradual fadeout to end

Strings

choo-ga choo-ga   choo-ga choo-ga   choo-ga choo-ga   *(Speaking)*

You Never Give Me Your Money

Words and Music by John Lennon and Paul McCartney

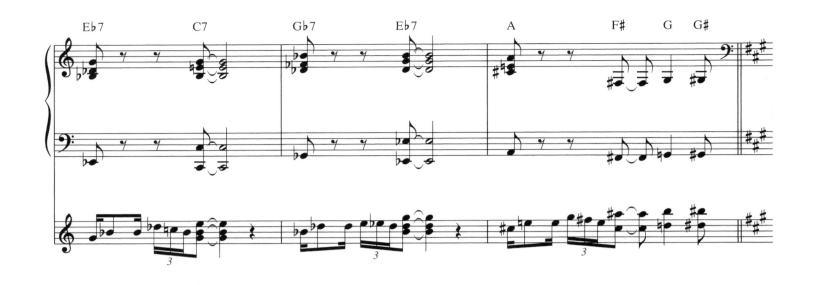

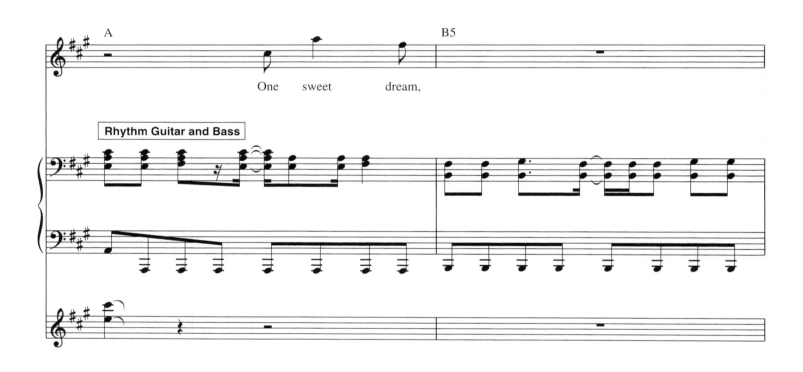

One sweet dream,

Rhythm Guitar and Bass

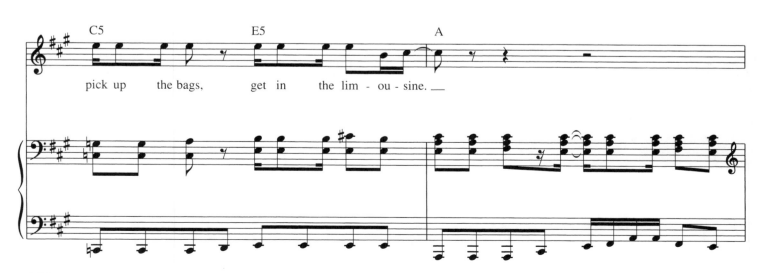

pick up the bags, get in the lim - ou - sine. __